Enjoy your Virginia History!

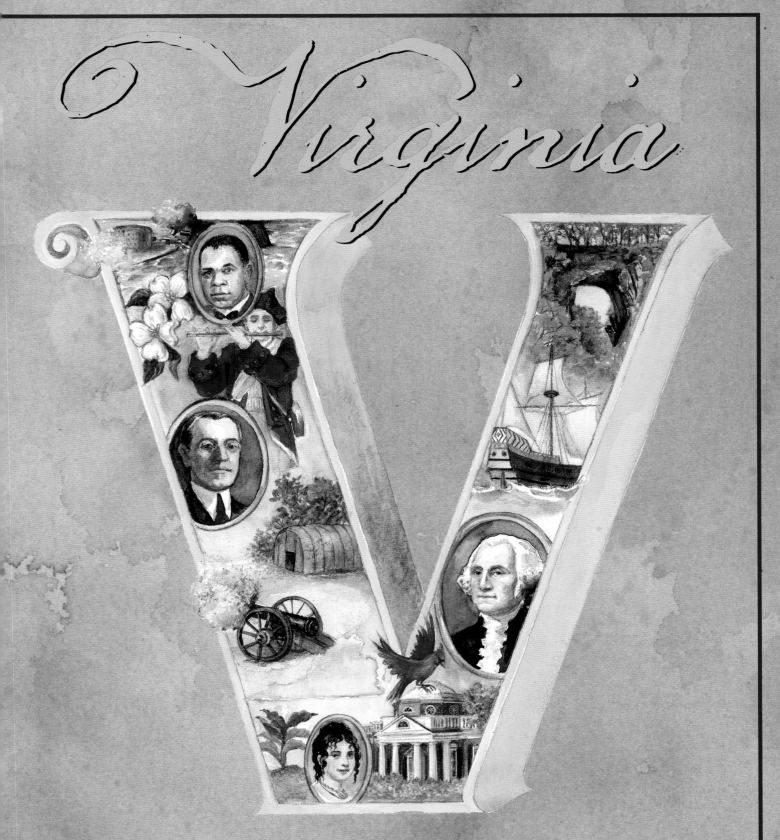

Virginia

AN ALPHABETICAL JOURNEY THROUGH HISTORY

Written by **Betty Bruce Shepard** *with* **Peter W. Barnes** *and* **Cheryl Shaw Barnes**

Illustrated by **Marsha Lederman**

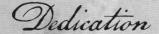

Dedication

To my grandchildren, Paige, Samantha, Emma Kate, and Maggie — four lovely young Virginia ladies — and to Landon, our little Virginia Gent.   — B.B.S.

To Zach and Genna.   — M.L.

Acknowledgments

We would like to thank our families and friends for their encouragement and patience during our long efforts to create this book. Thanks, also, to our readers and reviewers: Susie Orr, Fairfax County Public Schools elementary social studies specialist; Judy Santucci, FCPS elementary language arts specialist; and Ryan and Angela Graybill, 4th and 6th grade teachers, respectively, FCPS. We would also like to extend our appreciation to all the individuals and institutions throughout the Commonwealth who provided research assistance and expertise.

Shirley Gromen, Designer

Catherine Howell, Editor

Marsha Lederman, Art Director

Text copyright © 2007 by Betty Bruce Shepard
Illustrations copyright © 2007 by Marsha Lederman

ISBN 978-1-893622-14-2

Library of Congress Catalog Card number: 2006935149

10 9 8 7 6 5 4 3 2

Printed in the United States of America

Introduction

Virginia, the first permanent English settlement in North America, has a long and rich history. As you read through these pages, you will become aware of this and of the many connections that run through the Commonwealth's vital and varied past.

Due to the constraints of the illustrated alphabetical format, this book cannot offer a comprehensive presentation of the significant and interesting highlights of Virginia's historic people, places, and events. Choosing what to include was a difficult task, indeed! Also, historians sometimes differ with regard to facts and significance of events. We have taken this into account by consulting the most authoritative sources, recognizing, of course, that historical interpretation changes as new discoveries are made.

Virginia

ARLINGTON HOUSE sits high on a hill overlooking the Potomac River and Washington, D.C. Completed in 1818, it was the home of Robert E. Lee and his wife, Mary Custis Lee, a great-granddaughter of Martha Washington.

Mary Lee left Arlington House just after the start of the Civil War. When the Lees failed to pay taxes on the estate, the Union Army took it over. In 1864, the Army began to bury Union dead there, including in Mrs. Lee's rose garden. Confederate dead were buried on the grounds, too. The Union designated the property **ARLINGTON NATIONAL CEMETERY**. It is now the burial place for thousands of members of the armed services and their families — and for many famous Americans as well.

President John F. Kennedy and members of his family are buried here. The grave is marked by an eternal flame.

JAMES ARMISTEAD (1748?–1830), a slave owned by Virginia farmer William Armistead (slaves sometimes took their owner's name), served as a spy for French General Lafayette, who fought with the Americans during the Revolutionary War. James became a servant and guide for British General Lord Cornwallis, and passed on British military secrets to the Continental Army. Out of respect for the French hero, James later adopted Lafayette as his last name.

With Union forces bearing down on the Confederate Army, Union General Ulysses S. Grant and Confederate General Robert E. Lee met on April 9, 1865, in the parlor of the home of farmer Wilmer McLean in the small town of **APPOMATTOX COURT HOUSE** to end the Civil War. There, Grant and Lee agreed on the terms of the Confederate surrender. The leadership shown by these two courageous and dedicated men helped heal the country after four long years of conflict.

General Grant allowed Confederate soldiers to keep their horses or mules, and officers to also keep their guns. General Lee came dressed in his finest uniform, while Grant wore his old, mud-spattered one.

Richmond's **ARTHUR ASHE** (1943–1993) was the first African American man to become an international tennis champion. He helped to make tennis available and affordable for people of all races. Ashe spent much of his adult life working for education, fairness, and good health care for all.

Farmers and merchants founded **ALEXANDRIA** in 1749 on land owned by the Alexander family. It was an important seaport, busy with slave and tobacco trading and shipbuilding, and crowded with wharves, warehouses, and taverns. A young surveyor named George Washington helped plan the city's orderly layout.

Alexandria and its northern neighbor, ARLINGTON, were part of the nation's capital until the federal government returned them to Virginia in 1846.

Potomac River

This date stone, at right, appears over the side door of **BERKELEY**, a mansion built by Benjamin Harrison IV and his wife, Anne, on the James River. The 1726 completion date makes Berkeley the oldest three-story brick house in the state. The Harrisons' son Benjamin V signed the Declaration of Independence. Their grandson William Henry and great-great-grandson Benjamin VI became U.S. presidents.

Confederates: Grays, Rebels ("Rebs")

Union: Blues, Yankees ("Yanks")

The CIVIL WAR
(APRIL 12, 1861 – APRIL 9, 1865)

The Union and Confederate armies fought more than 380 battles during the **CIVIL WAR**. Many of them took place in Virginia because of the proximity of Washington, D.C., to Richmond, the capital of the Confederacy.

By the time Abraham Lincoln became president in 1861, Northern and Southern states had been arguing over slavery and states' rights for many years. By mid-June 1861, 11 Southern states, including Virginia, had seceded from the Union and formed the Confederate States of America. The first major battle of the war was fought at Manassas, at Bull Run Creek, in July 1861. Some of the last major battles were fought in Petersburg in 1865. The war ended that year, allowing the reunification of North and South. About a million Union and Confederate soldiers were wounded or died in the conflict, more casualties than in any other American war.

Politician **HARRY FLOOD BYRD** (1887–1966) from Winchester was a Virginia state senator, governor (1926–1930), and U.S. senator (1933–1965). During his governorship, Byrd approved a tax on gasoline to help pay for new highway construction. This became known as a "pay-as-you-go" program. During the 1950s, Byrd led the Massive Resistance movement that tried to stop black children from attending school with white children. Finally, in 1959, a few African American children enrolled in school with white students, the beginning of school integration.

Northern forces named battles for natural formations such as rivers or streams, while Southerners named them for towns or local landmarks such as churches.

Piedmont farmer **NATHANIEL BACON** (1647–1676) became angry when the royal governor, William Berkeley, would not help settlers in their battles with Virginia Indians. Berkeley wanted to maintain friendly relations with the Indians in order to trade with them. In 1676, Bacon led a revolt against Berkeley, who happened to be his cousin by marriage and had given him his land, which once belonged to the Indians. Bacon and his followers captured the capital of Jamestown, burning it and forcing the governor to flee. Bacon then fell ill suddenly and died, ending Bacon's Rebellion.

The CARDINAL was adopted by Virginia as state bird in 1950.

The **COMMONWEALTH OF VIRGINIA** is the state's official name, as declared by the Virginia Constitution adopted in June 1776. In a commonwealth, authority is held by the people united for the common good, or "common weal."

The **BLUE RIDGE MOUNTAINS** get their name from the hazy blue appearance of their tree-covered slopes when seen from a distance. They form the eastern edge of the great Appalachian range.

The James and Rappahannock Rivers begin in these mountains. They flow into the **CHESAPEAKE BAY**, along with the Potomac, York, and other rivers. The Bay is the largest estuary in the United States and flows into the Atlantic Ocean. The New River, which originates in these ancient mountains, may be one of the oldest rivers in North America.

Potomac River

Rappahannock River

Chesapeake Bay

Richmond ★

York River

James River

BLUE RIDGE MOUNTAINS

New River

RICHARD BYRD (1888–1957), Harry's brother, was a Navy officer, explorer, and aviator. He explored both the North and South Poles.

PEARL BAILEY (1918–1990) grew up in Newport News, where she started singing at age three in her father's church. A world-famous singer, she received many awards. In 1988, President Reagan awarded her the Medal of Freedom, the nation's highest civilian honor.

The BLUE CRAB is one of the Chesapeake Bay's 2,500 species of plants and animals.

The **GREAT DISMAL SWAMP**, located at the eastern border of Virginia and North Carolina, is the largest swamp in the Tidewater. It covers 111,000 acres and contains Lake Drummond, Virginia's largest natural lake. The name came from William Byrd II, a writer and wealthy landowner who led a team that surveyed the area in 1728. Byrd called the swamp "dreadful" and "dismal."

During the slavery period, fleeing slaves hid in the swamp. It was part of the Underground Railroad network that helped slaves escape to freedom in the North.

For Native Americans, early explorers, and settlers, the natural acids from organic materials in the swamp kept water pure and drinkable, even though it looked brown. It stayed fresh a long time in storage.

black bear

blue grosbeak

river otter

bobcat

spotted turtle

copperhead

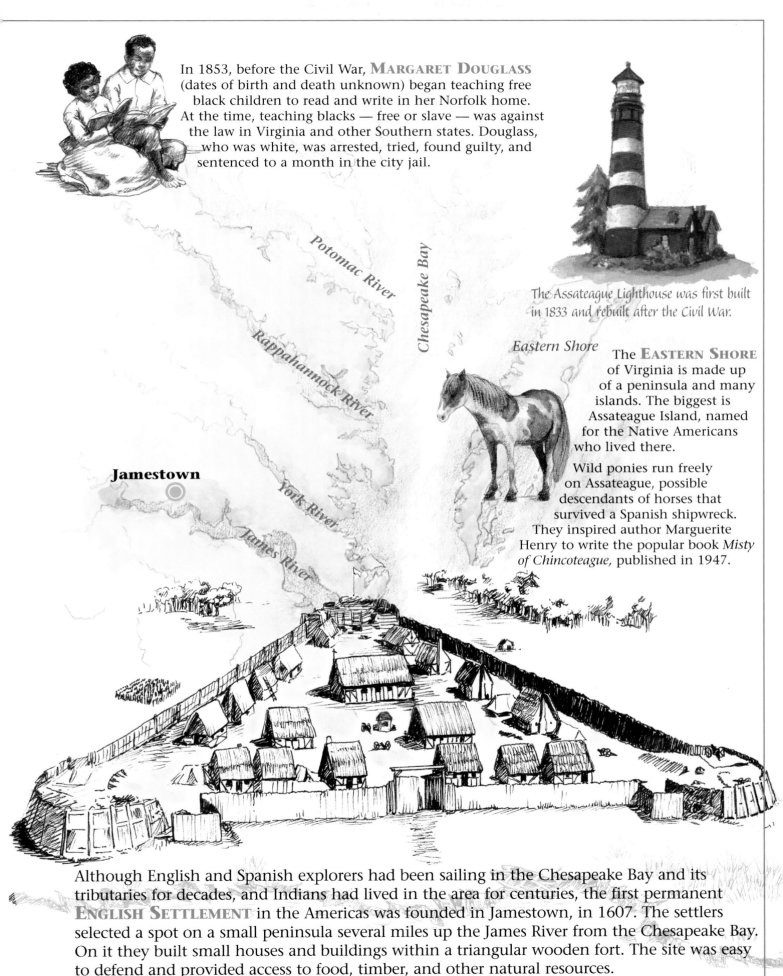

In 1853, before the Civil War, MARGARET DOUGLASS (dates of birth and death unknown) began teaching free black children to read and write in her Norfolk home. At the time, teaching blacks — free or slave — was against the law in Virginia and other Southern states. Douglass, who was white, was arrested, tried, found guilty, and sentenced to a month in the city jail.

The Assateague Lighthouse was first built in 1833 and rebuilt after the Civil War.

Eastern Shore

The EASTERN SHORE of Virginia is made up of a peninsula and many islands. The biggest is Assateague Island, named for the Native Americans who lived there.

Wild ponies run freely on Assateague, possible descendants of horses that survived a Spanish shipwreck. They inspired author Marguerite Henry to write the popular book *Misty of Chincoteague,* published in 1947.

Potomac River

Chesapeake Bay

Rappahannock River

Jamestown

York River

James River

Although English and Spanish explorers had been sailing in the Chesapeake Bay and its tributaries for decades, and Indians had lived in the area for centuries, the first permanent ENGLISH SETTLEMENT in the Americas was founded in Jamestown, in 1607. The settlers selected a spot on a small peninsula several miles up the James River from the Chesapeake Bay. On it they built small houses and buildings within a triangular wooden fort. The site was easy to defend and provided access to food, timber, and other natural resources.

In 1861, lawmakers chose the design of Virginia's **FLAG**, with the Great Seal of the Commonwealth in the middle. The seal incorporates Virginia's Latin motto, *Sic Semper Tyrannis*, meaning "Thus Always to Tyrants," or victory over tyranny. The seal itself was created in 1776 by a committee of Virginia patriots that included George Mason and George Wythe.

The FLOWERING DOGWOOD, a species native to Virginia, was adopted as the state flower in 1918 and the state tree in 1956.

FORT MYER in Arlington is the headquarters of one of the U.S. Army's oldest infantry units, The Old Guard, established in 1784. The fort also is home to the Army Band and a caisson platoon including more than 30 horses that pull caskets on the caissons to burial sites at Arlington National Cemetery. Members of The Old Guard keep watch around-the-clock at the cemetery's Tomb of the Unknowns.

FORT MONROE, named for President James Monroe, sits at the mouth of the James River and overlooks Hampton Roads, an important harbor. English colonists called this land Point Comfort, and built a fort here in 1609. Engineers began building the present fort in 1819. Robert E. Lee served as one of the construction supervisors. Jefferson Davis, president of the Confederacy, was held prisoner in the fort at the end of the Civil War.

The Old Point Comfort Lighthouse was commissioned by Thomas Jefferson and constructed in 1802.

During World Wars I and II, FORT MONROE guarded Hampton Roads from attack by enemy submarines.

FREDERICKSBURG was founded in 1728 at the falls of the Rappahannock River. It lies between Washington, D.C., and Richmond.

George Washington spent his childhood at Ferry Farm, located on the outskirts of Fredericksburg. The colonial house in the city that Washington purchased in 1772 for his mother, Mary, still stands there. Union and Confederate forces fought one of the most violent battles of the Civil War in Fredericksburg in 1862.

Fredericksburg

ELLA FITZGERALD (1918–1996) from Newport News was an internationally famous jazz singer. She is best known for her ability to improvise using rhythmic sounds and syllables instead of words, a technique called "scat singing." Ella received many awards, including 13 Grammys.

"A–Tisket, A–Tasket"

Virginia designated the AMERICAN FOXHOUND as the state dog in 1966. George Washington kept a pack of fine foxhounds descended from English dogs.

GUNSTON HALL, the plantation home of George Mason, is located on the Potomac River, a few miles downriver from Mount Vernon. George and his wife, Ann, planned and supervised the construction of this unique mansion, built circa 1755 to 1759. Unlike other homes of the period with just a few large bedrooms, Gunston Hall has seven small bedrooms on the second floor, which turned out to be wise planning — the Masons had nine children.

The Mason children and those of family and friends studied, danced, and enjoyed festive entertainment at Gunston Hall.

H and S

As a delegate to the second Virginia Convention at St. John's Church in Richmond, Henry gave a famous speech on March 23, 1775, supporting independence for the colony. It ended with the declaration, "I know not what course others may take; but as for me, give me liberty or give me death!"

PATRICK HENRY (1736–1799), born in Hanover County in the Piedmont, was a self-taught lawyer who became a persuasive public speaker and politician. He was elected to the House of Burgesses in 1765 and later was delegate to the Continental Congress. Henry was elected as Virginia's first governor in 1776. Ironically, he lived in the Governor's Palace in Williamsburg, the building that represented the English rule he hated so much. He served as governor again in the 1780s.

In the early 19th century, **HARPERS FERRY** (a part of Virginia at that time and now part of West Virginia) was the site of a large government weapons factory and stockpile. In 1859, radical abolitionist John Brown and his followers seized the armory and the arsenal. Brown hoped to encourage slaves to rebel against their owners and join him in a free black republic in the Appalachian Mountains. But slaves did not revolt, and Brown was captured, tried, and hanged for his actions.

U.S. AMMU...

Harpers Ferry

In 1863, western Virginia refused to join the Confederacy and separated from Virginia, becoming the state of West Virginia.

"Achoo!"

President Harrison refused to wear a hat or coat to his inauguration, despite the cold and rainy weather. He developed pneumonia and died a month later!

President Harrison
1773 – 1841

WILLIAM HENRY HARRISON was born on his grandfather's estate, Berkeley Plantation in the Tidewater. He studied to become a doctor but joined the U.S. Army after his father died. He gained fame as a successful general in the Indian wars in the 1800s. Before becoming president, Harrison was also a congressman and senator. His grandson Benjamin was the 23rd president.

9TH PRESIDENT (March – April 1841)

★ Harrison took office at age 68 (the oldest man to become president up to that time), earning him the nickname "Old Granny."

★ His inaugural address lasted almost two hours, the longest in U.S. history.

★ He became the first president to die in office, after only a month, the shortest term in U.S. history. He was succeeded by his vice president, John Tyler, a fellow Virginian.

The James and Elizabeth Rivers flow into **HAMPTON ROADS**, a large natural harbor, and out into the Chesapeake Bay and the Atlantic Ocean beyond it. President George Washington commissioned America's first lighthouse, the Old Cape Henry Lighthouse (right), at nearby Virginia Beach. It was built from sandstone block from 1791 to 1792. When it began to crack, a second lighthouse (left) was built in 1881 and is still in use.

During the Civil War, Confederate troops broke the beacon in the Old Cape Henry Lighthouse to make navigation dangerous for Union ships.

In the waters of **HAMPTON ROADS**, two ironclad ships engaged in a famous Civil War naval battle on March 9, 1862. The Union's *Monitor* and the Confederacy's *Virginia* (the rebuilt *Merrimack*) fought for more than three hours. The battle ended in a draw and neither ship received much damage.

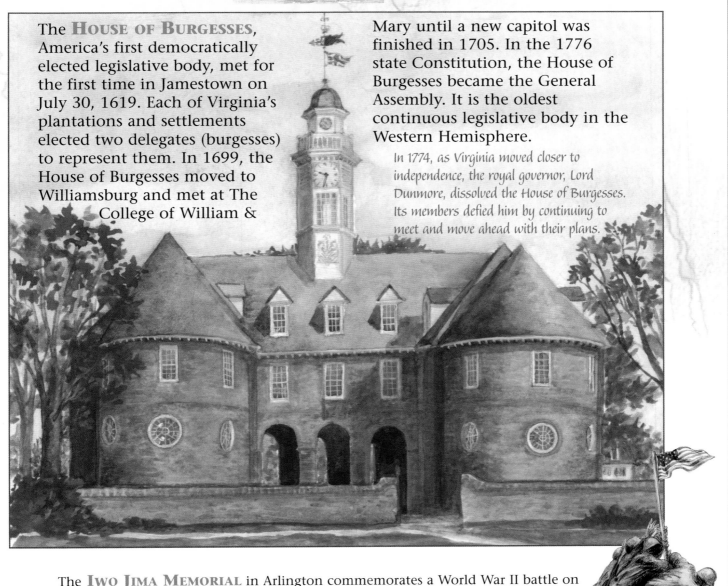

The **HOUSE OF BURGESSES**, America's first democratically elected legislative body, met for the first time in Jamestown on July 30, 1619. Each of Virginia's plantations and settlements elected two delegates (burgesses) to represent them. In 1699, the House of Burgesses moved to Williamsburg and met at The College of William & Mary until a new capitol was finished in 1705. In the 1776 state Constitution, the House of Burgesses became the General Assembly. It is the oldest continuous legislative body in the Western Hemisphere.

In 1774, as Virginia moved closer to independence, the royal governor, Lord Dunmore, dissolved the House of Burgesses. Its members defied him by continuing to meet and move ahead with their plans.

The **IWO JIMA MEMORIAL** in Arlington commemorates a World War II battle on the Japanese island of Iwo Jima. The memorial, dedicated in 1954, serves as the official tribute to the United States Marine Corps. The statue design is based on a famous photograph showing Marines and a Navy corpsman raising the American flag on Mount Suribachi, the island's highest point.

In April 1607, 100 men and four boys sailed into the Chesapeake Bay from England in three ships. They were sent by the Virginia Company of London, which hoped they would find gold and silver in the New World. A month later, they built a fort on the banks of a river and named both the river and the settlement **JAMESTOWN**, in honor of their king, James I.

Many of the colonists were English gentlemen with few practical or survival skills. Others were craftsman and laborers, while some were indentured servants — laborers under contract who could earn their freedom after working for a set number of years. By September, their supplies were gone and more than half the colonists had died from starvation or disease.

The settlers built their first houses in the English style of the time, using "wattle," wooden strips woven over and under horizontal branches or stakes. They covered this with a mixture of clay, sand, straw, and water called "daub." They topped the structures with thatched roofs.

Maintaining good health and steady food supplies remained a challenge, as did keeping good relations with the Virginia Indians whose land and food colonists usually took without permission. Some Indian tribes wanted to trade with the colonists. Others were angry with the colonists' desire for more food and more land to settle and farm. Bloody fighting occurred many times. Despite all this, Jamestown survived, grew, and eventually prospered. Within a few decades, Virginia was Britain's wealthiest and most successful colony in the Americas. In May 2007, Jamestown marked its 400th Anniversary.

The Godspeed, the Susan Constant, and the Discovery brought the first permanent English settlers to the New World.

Captain Smith explored and mapped the Chesapeake Bay and its rivers.

CAPTAIN JOHN SMITH — an experienced soldier with common sense — was Virginia's first important English leader. He established a good relationship with Powhatan, the paramount chief of many of the coastal Virginia Indians. Powhatan traded food to Smith for glass beads, copper pots, and other English goods. Smith was accidentally burned by gunpowder in 1609 and returned to England, never to see Jamestown again.

In 1608, the first two women, Mrs. Thomas Forrest and her maid, Anne Burris, arrived in Jamestown. A few more women came in 1609. In 1620, a "bride ship" brought about 90 more women to the settlement. Some hoped to marry, others came as indentured servants, and still others were wives of colonists who wanted to join their husbands in establishing a new life.

In 1619, British pirates traded about 20 Africans to the colonists for food and water. These first Africans in the settlement had been captured in southwestern Africa. In Jamestown they probably were made indentured servants. But many more Africans were later forced into slavery in English colonies.

President Jefferson

1743 – 1826

THOMAS JEFFERSON

was born on a farm in what is now Albemarle County in the Piedmont. At 16, he enrolled in The College of William & Mary. After completing his studies there, he read law for five years with George Wythe. He married Martha Skelton in 1772 and they had six children, but only two lived to adulthood. Martha died in 1782 and Jefferson never remarried.

Jefferson started his political career in the House of Burgesses. During the Revolutionary period, he was a representative to the Continental Congress and wrote the Declaration of Independence and the Virginia Statute for Religious Freedom. He also served as governor of Virginia. After the Revolution, Jefferson became minister to France, the nation's first secretary of state, and vice president under President John Adams.

Jefferson was also a scientist, inventor, architect, educator, farmer, and gardener. He designed and redesigned his beautiful home, Monticello. He founded the University of Virginia, planning its buildings and writing the curricula.

Jefferson died at Monticello on July 4, 1826, 50 years after the adoption of the Declaration of Independence. Despite his many accomplishments, he requested that only three be inscribed on his tombstone: his authorship of the Declaration and of the Statute for Religious Freedom, and his founding of the University of Virginia.

3RD PRESIDENT (1801 – 1809)

★ Jefferson was the first president to be inaugurated in Washington, D.C.

★ He was the first president to shake hands instead of bowing to people, and the first not to wear a powdered wig.

★ His daughter Martha (nicknamed "Patsy") served as first lady. One of her sons was the first child born in the President's House.

★ He completed the Louisiana Purchase in 1803, doubling the country's size.

THOMAS "STONEWALL" JACKSON (1824–1863) graduated from the U.S. Military Academy at West Point, New York. He was a professor of military tactics and also taught science at the Virginia Military Institute in Lexington. When Virginia seceded from the Union, he joined the Confederate Army and became one of General Robert E. Lee's most devoted commanders. Jackson was shot accidentally by his own troops at Chancellorsville and died eight days later.

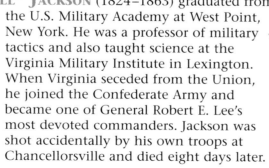

STONEWALL JACKSON

During the First Battle of Manassas, another commander pointed to the general and shouted, "Look, men! There is Jackson standing like a stone wall...!"

Jefferson improved a copying machine, the polygraph, which duplicated a document as it was being handwritten.

The JAMESTOWN GLASSHOUSE, established in 1608, was America's first factory.

KENMORE in Fredericksburg is a historic brick manor house. It was built in the 1770s by George Washington's only sister, Betty, and her husband, Fielding Lewis.

ROBERT E. LEE

(1807–1870) was born at Stratford Hall, his family's plantation on the Potomac River in Westmoreland County. He was the fourth generation of one of Virginia's most famous, active, and influential families. As a child, he lived in Alexandria. He attended the U.S. Military Academy at West Point, New York (where he later served as superintendent), and fought in the Mexican-American War.

Lee married Mary Custis, George Washington's great-granddaughter, and lived in her family home, Arlington House. At the onset of the Civil War, Lee refused President Lincoln's offer to command the Union Army. Although he opposed slavery and had freed his own slaves, he did not want to fight against his home state. By 1862, he was commander of the Army of Northern Virginia, the Confederacy's main fighting force.

Located in the beautiful mountain town of **LEXINGTON** are the Virginia Military Institute, founded in 1839, and Washington and Lee University, established in 1782 as Liberty Hall Academy. The University's current name honors George Washington, who made a donation to help the school, and Robert E. Lee, who was its president after the Civil War.

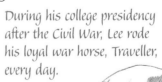

During his college presidency after the Civil War, Lee rode his loyal war horse, Traveller, every day.

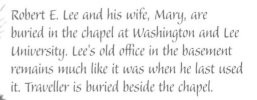

Robert E. Lee and his wife, Mary, are buried in the chapel at Washington and Lee University. Lee's old office in the basement remains much like it was when he last used it. Traveller is buried beside the chapel.

Expedition Route

LOUISIANA TERRITORY

Lewis and Clark hired a French Canadian trapper and his Indian wife, Sacagawea, as interpreters. Sacagawea made the trip carrying her baby boy on her back. She saved maps, notebooks, and instruments when a large canoe capsized.

Seaman, Lewis's Newfoundland dog, was large, furry, and brave. He once scared off a bison charging into camp.

Native Americans were fascinated with Clark's slave York, the only African American member of the expedition.

Pacific Ocean

Clark

Lewis

The expedition, called the Corps of Discovery, started with more than 40 men, most of them U.S. Army soldiers.

MERIWETHER LEWIS (1774–1809) was born near Charlottesville. His mentor, Thomas Jefferson, appointed him his personal secretary in 1801, when Jefferson became president. After Jefferson acquired the **LOUISIANA TERRITORY** from France in 1803, he commissioned Lewis to explore this vast, unmapped area. The Louisiana Purchase doubled the size of the young nation, greatly increasing its natural and economic resources.

Lewis asked his friend, **WILLIAM CLARK** (1770–1838) from the Tidewater region, to lead the expedition with him. One of Clark's responsibilities was to keep a daily journal that included drawings and maps. Lewis collected samples of plants and animals, fossils, and other items, and kept detailed notes. The journey began in May 1804 and lasted more than two years, taking the explorers to the Pacific Ocean and back, a round trip of 8,000 miles.

LURAY CAVERNS in the Valley and Ridge region is one of several limestone cave systems in this area. Large open rooms and spectacular rock formations fill the caverns.

Icicle-like stalactites hang down from cavern walls and ceilings.

Stalagmites grow upward from cavern floors.

The explorers called the unfamiliar prairie dogs "barking squirrels." They sent one back to President Jefferson.

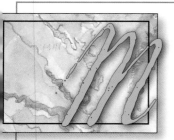

GEORGE MASON (1725–1792) was born in what is now Fairfax County into a family of wealthy landowners. Though he never formally studied law, he read a lot about it, and was active in his community, winning election to the House of Burgesses. In 1775, Mason began to attend Virginia conventions and worked toward gaining independence from Great Britain. He drafted the Virginia Constitution and helped write the Virginia Declaration of Rights. But Mason refused to sign the U.S. Constitution because he felt it gave too much power to the federal government, did not end the importation of slaves, and lacked a national declaration of citizens' rights.

This statue of George Mason is in Washington, D.C.

Mason's leadership and writings helped bring about the addition of the Bill of Rights to the U.S. Constitution.

President Madison

1751 – 1836

Madison was the smallest president, standing slightly more than five feet tall and never weighing more than 150 pounds. He had a weak voice but a brilliant mind. When he spoke, people listened!

JAMES MADISON grew up in Orange County at Montpelier, his family's plantation. He attended the College of New Jersey (later called Princeton) and graduated in 1771. As a delegate to the Virginia Convention in 1776, he assisted George Mason in drafting Virginia's Constitution and the Virginia Declaration of Rights. Later that year, he joined the newly created House of Delegates. Madison was a vocal leader at the Constitutional Convention in 1787 and was the principal author of the U.S. Constitution. He favored a strong central government, but with a system of checks and balances through three separate branches — executive, legislative, and judicial. Madison co-authored The Federalist Papers, more than 80 articles that argued for the Constitution's ratification. During George Washington's presidency, Madison served in the U.S. House of Representatives and wrote the Bill of Rights, the first ten amendments to the Constitution. He served as secretary of state for Thomas Jefferson.

4th President (1809 – 1817)

★ Madison was our first war-time president, leading America through the War of 1812. Although British troops entered Washington and burned the President's House, the Capitol, and other government buildings, he proved that a democratic country could successfully go to war.

★ He became known as the "Father of the Constitution," a title he did not like.

DOLLEY PAYNE TODD MADISON (1768–1849), a well-educated young woman raised a Quaker in Richmond and Philadelphia, married James Madison in 1794. As first lady, Dolley set the capital's standards for fashion, manners, and entertainment. After her husband died, she left Montpelier to return to Washington, where she remained active in social and political life until her death.

When the British burned the President's House in 1814 (during the War of 1812), Dolley's quick thinking and actions saved a portrait of George Washington and some important papers. Fleeing the house, she grabbed silver from the dining room and stuffed it in her reticule, or handbag.

MONTPELIER was the Madison family home and plantation. The central brick portion of the house was built in about 1760 by James Madison's father. With advice from his friend Thomas Jefferson, James renovated the house twice, adding a front portico, or porch, and two one-story wings. James and Dolley lived there for nearly 20 years after his presidency.

MOUNT VERNON, the home of George Washington, overlooks the Potomac River in Fairfax County, about 15 miles south of Washington, D.C. George's father likely built the first part of the house in the 1730s. After he died in 1743, George's half brother, Lawrence, moved there. Lawrence had been an officer in the British Navy and renamed the estate in honor of his commander, Admiral Edward Vernon.

George inherited the property in 1761. He added a full second story to the house and a high-columned porch covering its entire width on the river side. In 1860, a group of concerned women bought the plantation and rescued it from neglect. The estate has been restored to its appearance at the time George and his wife, Martha, lived there.

MONTICELLO, the home of Thomas Jefferson, was his architectural masterpiece, designed and redesigned throughout his adult life. Constructed on a mountaintop near Charlottesville, Monticello is Italian for "Little Mountain." The mansion, with its distinctive central dome, has 33 rooms and is filled with practical inventions and furniture designed by Jefferson.

Recognized as an international treasure, Monticello is listed by the United Nations as a World Heritage site.

JOHN MARSHALL (1755–1835) was born in what is now Fauquier County and became an officer in the Continental Army, serving with George Washington. A member of the Virginia legislature, he later became secretary of state for President John Adams. In 1801, Adams appointed Marshall the fourth Chief Justice of the Supreme Court. His rulings and leadership helped establish the U.S. Constitution as the supreme law of the land.

President Monroe
1758 – 1831

JAMES MONROE

was born on a farm in Westmoreland County in the Tidewater. At age 17, he joined the Continental Army, serving under George Washington. He studied law with Thomas Jefferson, who became a lifelong friend. In 1789, Monroe and his wife, Elizabeth, moved to Charlottesville, where they built a plantation near Jefferson's Monticello. (They called it Highland, but it was renamed Ash Lawn by a later owner.). Monroe served as governor of Virginia, minister to France, and secretary of state. He died on July 4, 1831.

5TH PRESIDENT (1817 – 1825)

★ Monroe ran unopposed in the election of 1820. George Washington was the only other president without an election opponent.

★ He was the last president from the Revolutionary War era and had been wounded in battle — a bullet in his shoulder was never removed.

★ He moved back into the rebuilt President's House, which had been burned in the War of 1812. He reopened it to the public on New Year's Day in 1818.

★ He announced the Monroe Doctrine in 1823. It declared that European nations should not establish new colonies in the Western Hemisphere and should not meddle in its affairs.

OLD DOMINION is Virginia's nickname. It referred to Virginia's status as England's oldest colony in the New World and placed it among the king's other overseas dominions in the 17th century.

When the English arrived in Virginia in 1607, an estimated 14,000 to 21,000 Algonquian-speaking **NATIVE VIRGINIA INDIANS** lived in the Tidewater. Some of these tribes were members of Powhatan's paramount chiefdom, made up of more than 30 tribes in more than 150 towns and villages. Two other tribal nations in the coastal region spoke dialects of the Iroquoian language. Many Siouan-speaking tribes lived in the Piedmont region. The Cherokee, of the Iroquoian language group, lived to the West in the Valley and Ridge region and on the Appalachian Plateau. Virginia's Indians often fought with colonists to protect their land and way of life, and over time, many Indians were killed, died from disease, or left due to loss of their land. Some Indians remained, living on reservations or in their own communities. Today, Virginia's Indian population includes members of the eight different tribes recognized by the state.

At the time of English settlement, a Powhatan village was made up of a few families to a few hundred families, living in houses called yehakins in Algonquian, some small and round, others large and oblong.

NATURAL BRIDGE, near Lexington in the Valley and Ridge, is an immense stone bridge formed when water eroded soft rock over millions of years. During the Revolution, a French engineer measured the bridge at 215$\frac{1}{2}$ feet high (as high as a 17-story building).

Some believe George Washington surveyed the bridge and carved his initials in the rock. In 1774, Thomas Jefferson acquired it as part of a land purchase.

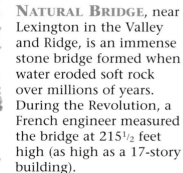

Virginia Indian
circa 1585

When the English arrived in Virginia, **POWHATAN** (circa 1547–1618) was the paramount chief of many tribes. He initially welcomed the newcomers and established an important trading relationship with one of the early Jamestown leaders, Captain John Smith, exchanging food for English goods. The food helped the colony to survive.

Pocahontas and her son, Thomas Rolfe, in England.

POCAHONTAS (circa 1595–1617) was a daughter of Powhatan. According to Captain John Smith, she saved him by pleading for his life after her father had ordered him killed, although many historians doubt this account. Kidnapped by the English in 1614, she accepted conversion to Christianity — taking the name Rebecca — and marriage to colonist John Rolfe. The couple had a son, Thomas. This marriage brought several years of peace between the colonists and the Indians. In 1616, the Rolfe family went to England, where Pocahontas was treated like royalty. She became ill on a ship returning to Virginia, was taken back to England, and died there. Pocahontas is buried in Gravesend, England.

MARY PEAKE (1823–1862) was a free-born African American from Norfolk. She married Thomas Peake of Hampton, who was a spy for the Union during the Civil War. Mary was one of the first African American teachers in the South. She secretly taught black children and adults, both free and slave, to read and write.

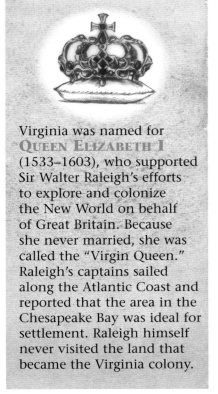

Virginia was named for **QUEEN ELIZABETH I** (1533–1603), who supported Sir Walter Raleigh's efforts to explore and colonize the New World on behalf of Great Britain. Because she never married, she was called the "Virgin Queen." Raleigh's captains sailed along the Atlantic Coast and reported that the area in the Chesapeake Bay was ideal for settlement. Raleigh himself never visited the land that became the Virginia colony.

The **PENTAGON** in Arlington County is named for its five-sided design. With more than six million square feet of space on 29 acres, it is one of the largest office buildings in the world, serving as headquarters for the U.S. Department of Defense. The government completed construction of the Pentagon in 1943 during World War II. On September 11, 2001, the Pentagon was struck by a jet plane in a terrorist attack that killed or injured many people. The damaged part was rebuilt, rededicated, and reopened within a year.

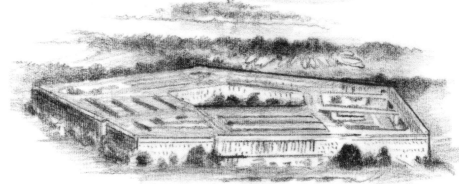

The 13 American colonies fought for their independence from Great Britain in the **REVOLUTIONARY WAR** (1775–1783). In this conflict, the colonists known as patriots were upset with England's treatment of the colonies, which included demands for taxes and British restrictions on self-government. Loyalist colonists remained faithful to England and King George III.

Many people on both sides hoped to settle the disputes peacefully. But after a number of harsh actions by the British against Virginia and other colonies, the patriots prevailed. In 1776, Virginia sent Thomas Jefferson, George Wythe, and other delegates to the Continental Congress in Philadelphia to formally declare independence from England. A Virginian, Richard Henry Lee, presented the resolution.

In the war, many Virginians fought in the Continental Army, led by Virginian George Washington. Others provided soldiers with food, clothing, and supplies. Some loyalists left Virginia. Until 1781, few battles were fought in Virginia. But the conflict concluded there when American and French forces trapped the British Army in Yorktown. England's commanding general, Lord Cornwallis, surrendered on October 19, 1781. The war officially ended with the Treaty of Paris in 1783. The Americans' victory allowed them to form a free, self-governing United States.

Continental soldiers wore different types of uniforms — when they could get them. The uniforms often were drab and tattered. Some soldiers wore shoes with holes in them, or no shoes at all.

British grenadiers (specially trained foot soldiers) were recognized by their distinctive and colorful uniforms.

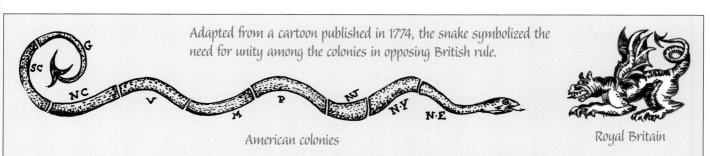

Adapted from a cartoon published in 1774, the snake symbolized the need for unity among the colonies in opposing British rule.

American colonies

Royal Britain

JAMES EWELL BROWN "J.E.B." STUART
(1833–1864) was born near the Blue Ridge Mountains and graduated from the U.S. Military Academy at West Point, New York. In 1861, he resigned from the U. S. Army to join the Confederate Army. As the commanding general of the Confederate cavalry, he earned recognition as a brilliant leader and valuable spy. Stuart was wounded in a battle outside Richmond in 1864, and died a few days later.

J.E.B. Stuart was known as the "eyes and ears" of the Confederate Army.

RICHMOND became Virginia's capital in 1780, when the capital was relocated from Williamsburg due to the threat of British attack during the Revolutionary War. The General Assembly, consisting of the House of Delegates and the Senate, met in a tobacco merchant's store until a new capitol building was completed. During the Civil War, Richmond was the capital of the Confederacy.

The state capitol, designed by Thomas Jefferson, was constructed between 1785 and 1798. Modeled after a Roman temple, it was the first building in America erected in this classical style. Virginia's capitol is the second oldest in continuous use in the United States and houses the Western Hemisphere's oldest continuous legislative body. The state completed a renovation of the capitol in May 2007.

circa 1790

As Union troops marched on Richmond at the end of the Civil War, fleeing Confederate soldiers set fire to buildings and warehouses on April 3, 1865, to keep supplies out of enemy hands — but they did not burn the capitol.

The SKYLINE DRIVE begins in Front Royal and extends about 100 miles across the top of the Blue Ridge Mountains. The highway, built in the 1930s, offers travelers beautiful panoramic views.

Skyline Drive

MOUNT ROGERS, 5,729 feet above sea level, is the highest peak in Virginia.

During the Civil War, former slave Mary Bowser was a member of a Richmond **SPY RING** that collected information about Confederate activities for the Union. The ring's leader was Elizabeth Van Lew, a wealthy resident who had been Mary's owner. Elizabeth had freed Mary and arranged for her education. She then got Mary a job as a servant at the Confederate White House, where President Jefferson Davis worked. Pretending to be unintelligent, Mary paid attention to documents and conversations and passed on the details to Union informants.

SHIRLEY, Virginia's first plantation, was founded in 1613 on the James River. It is the oldest working plantation in North America and has been owned by the Hill and Carter families for 11 generations. Constructed between 1723 and 1738, the mansion has identical entrances, one facing the river and the other facing inland.

Revolutionary War Captain Jack Jouett of Albemarle County was known as the **PAUL REVERE OF THE SOUTH**. On June 3, 1781, Jouett spotted 250 British soldiers near a tavern in Louisa County and rode 40 miles through the night to warn Governor Thomas Jefferson of their approach. Jouett's action allowed Jefferson and other Virginia leaders to escape capture.

WALTER REED (1851–1902) from Gloucester County studied medicine at the University of Virginia and became a U.S. Army surgeon. In Cuba after the Spanish-American War, Reed determined that yellow fever was transmitted by mosquitoes. That disease and others had killed more soldiers than the fighting during the war. Reed's discovery helped limit the disease through controls on mosquito breeding.

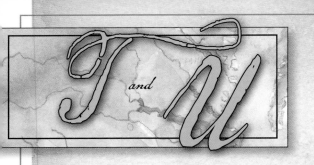

The founding of **UNIVERSITY OF VIRGINIA** in Charlottesville in 1819 was one of Thomas Jefferson's proudest accomplishments. He designed the university's original buildings, modeling the Rotunda after the Pantheon in Rome. Jefferson also wrote the program of studies, hired the faculty, and selected the library books. He watched the construction from his nearby mountaintop home, Monticello. Along with Monticello, the University of Virginia has been designated a World Heritage site.

President Tyler
1790 – 1862

JOHN TYLER

grew up on an estate in Charles City County in the Tidewater, graduated from The College of William & Mary, and became a lawyer and politician. He was a member of the Virginia House of Delegates, a U.S. congressman, and Virginia's governor. He was elected a U.S. senator in 1827 and vice president in 1840. During the Civil War, he became active again in Virginia politics, and was the only former president to renounce his U.S. citizenship and join the Confederacy.

10TH PRESIDENT (1841–1845)

★ Tyler was the first vice president to become president upon the death of a chief executive. He was sworn in two days after the death of William Henry Harrison, a fellow Virginian. Tyler served his single term without a vice president, the only president to do so.

★ He was the first president to marry while in office. His first wife, Letitia, had died and he remarried, to Julia Gardiner.

★ With Letitia and Julia, he was the father of 15 children, the most of any president.

TOBACCO, also called Golden Weed, was the colony's main source of income.

Jamestown colonist John Rolfe experimented with **TOBACCO** plants from the West Indies, producing a sweeter strain than the native tobacco grown and used by local Indians. England's demand for this new tobacco made it the colony's most profitable export. Because gold and silver were scarce in Virginia, colonists also used tobacco as currency, to purchase food and other goods

The Tylers were famous for their parties and introduced the polka to the White House. During retirement at his plantation, Sherwood Hall, Tyler enjoyed playing the violin, often accompanied by Julia, who played the guitar or sang.

Though born in Virginia, Taylor was elected president from Louisiana, the first president elected from west of the Mississippi.

President Taylor
1784 – 1850

Virginia designated the TIGER SWALLOWTAIL as state insect in 1991.

ZACHARY TAYLOR

was born on a farm in Orange County in the Piedmont. In 1808, he was commissioned as an officer in the U.S. Army and spent 40 years in military service. A courageous soldier and commander, Taylor fought in the War of 1812 and the Mexican-American War. His nickname was "Old Rough and Ready."

12TH PRESIDENT (1849–1850)

★ Taylor was the first president who never had held any previous political office. He had never even voted in a presidential election!

★ The controversy over slavery was a major issue during his administration. Taylor, who owned slaves, threatened military action against any southern state that tried to secede over the issue of slavery.

★ He died suddenly in Washington, D.C., after 16 months in office.

★ His horse, Old Whitey, walked behind his casket in the funeral procession. The riderless horse represented the loss of a great leader.

Old Whitey was allowed to roam and graze on the White House lawn.

NAT TURNER (1800–1831) was born a slave in Southampton County in the Tidewater. Able to read and write, he was deeply religious and preached to fellow slaves. Saying he was inspired by God, he led a group of slaves in a bloody rebellion in August 1831 against his master and other slaveholders, killing about 60 of them. Turner and his followers were arrested and executed, but the incident brought national attention to the issue of abolishing slavery.

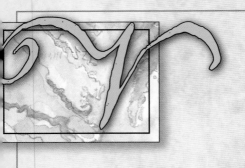

VIRGINIA ratified the U.S. Constitution on June 25, 1788. It was the tenth state to ratify the document. Virginia and Virginians have played important roles in the nation's history:

- "Mother of Presidents" — eight presidents were born in Virginia, including four of the first five.

- Seven signers of the Declaration of Independence came from Virginia, more than from any other colony: George Wythe, Richard Henry Lee, Thomas Jefferson, Benjamin Harrison, Thomas Nelson Jr., Francis Lightfoot Lee, and Carter Braxton.

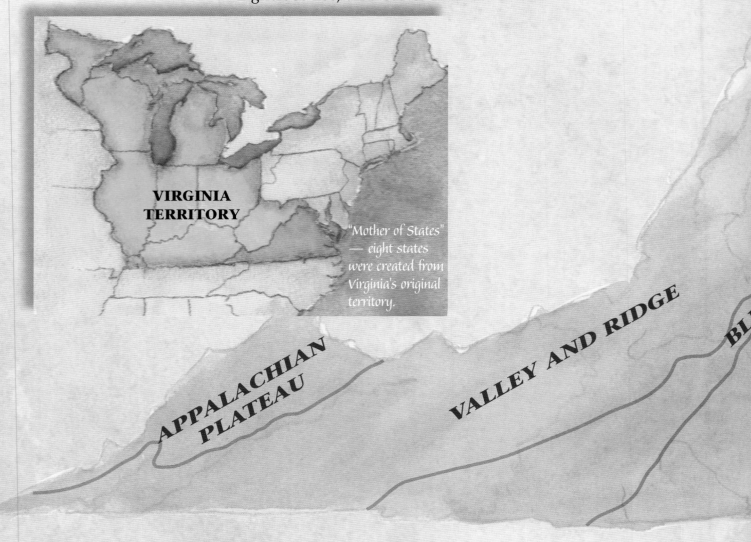

VIRGINIA TERRITORY

"Mother of States" — eight states were created from Virginia's original territory.

APPALACHIAN PLATEAU

VALLEY AND RIDGE

BL

Virginia's neighbors are Maryland, West Virginia, Kentucky, Tennessee, North Carolina, and the District of Columbia.

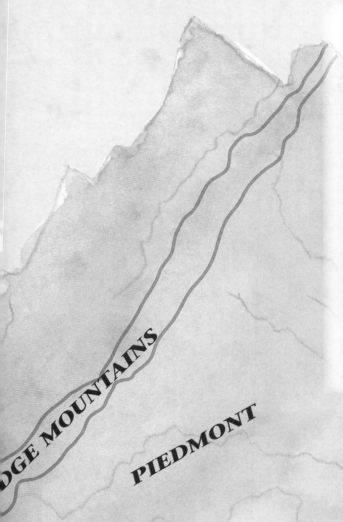

VIRGINIA has five distinct geographic regions. The flat coastal plain is called the **Tidewater**. It is formed by the four great tidal rivers — the Potomac, Rappahannock, York, and James — which flow into the Chesapeake Bay and out into the Atlantic Ocean.

Westward, the Tidewater rises to the **fall line** through Richmond and becomes the rolling, fertile land of the **Piedmont**.

The Piedmont climbs to the **Blue Ridge Mountains**, a region that is part of the Appalachian Mountain range.

Farther west, in the **Valley and Ridge** region, gentle valleys separate forested mountain ridges. The Shenandoah Valley is the most famous.

In the southwestern corner of the state is the **Appalachian Plateau** region.

The **VIRGINIA DECLARATION OF RIGHTS** was written by George Mason in 1776 as part of the new Constitution adopted that year by Virginia's revolutionary leaders. The document set forth basic liberties, such as freedom of the press and the right to vote. The first 10 amendments to the U.S. Constitution, known as the Bill of Rights, are based on this Declaration.

The **VIRGINIA STATUTE FOR RELIGIOUS FREEDOM** established freedom of religion for Virginia citizens and emphasized the separation of church and state. This statute, authored by Thomas Jefferson, was adopted in 1786 and became the basis for the First Amendment to the U.S. Constitution.

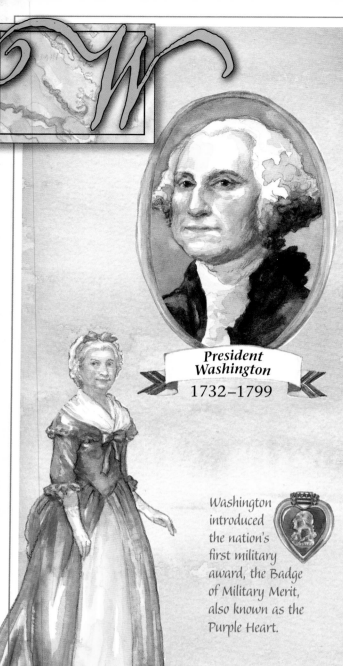

President Washington
1732–1799

Washington introduced the nation's first military award, the Badge of Military Merit, also known as the Purple Heart.

GEORGE WASHINGTON is called the "Father of Our Country" because of his military and political leadership during the American Revolution and the formation of the United States. Washington was born on Pope's Creek Plantation in Westmoreland County in the Tidewater. In his early years, he worked as a surveyor, justice of the peace, and farmer. Self-educated, he never attended college.

Washington served in the Virginia militia, but left in 1758 to become a planter and politician. He was elected to the House of Burgesses at age 26. The next year, he married Martha Custis, a widow with two children, and they moved to Mount Vernon.

In 1775, Washington was appointed commander in chief of the Continental Army and led the colonies in their fight for independence from England. He served as the presiding officer of the Constitutional Convention in Philadelphia in 1787, and was elected the new nation's first president in 1789.

In 1797, after two terms as president, Washington retired to his beloved Mount Vernon. He died there on December 14, 1799, of a severe throat infection two days after a horseback ride in sleet and snow. In his will, Washington freed his slaves.

1ST PRESIDENT (1789–1797)

★ Washington was unanimously elected president for both terms.

★ He was inaugurated in New York City, and was the only president who did not live in the President's House (later called the White House).

★ His presidency focused on organizing and implementing the new government.

MARTHA DANDRIDGE CUSTIS WASHINGTON (1731–1802) was America's first first lady. Born near Williamsburg, Martha was a wealthy widow with two toddlers when she married George Washington in 1759. Martha and George were devoted parents, raising the children — and later, two grandchildren — at Mount Vernon. During the Revolutionary War, Martha traveled long distances and shared many hardships with her husband. Martha was a true lady — refined, always dignified and gracious, yet warm and hospitable, making everyone feel comfortable.

GEORGE WYTHE (1726–1806), born in Tidewater, was a lawyer and judge, and served in the House of Burgesses. A signer of the Declaration of Independence, Wythe also helped draft the Virginia Constitution. He counted Thomas Jefferson, John Marshall, and James Monroe among his famous law students. In 1779, Governor Jefferson appointed Wythe the nation's first academic law professor, at The College of William & Mary.

L. DOUGLAS WILDER (1931–), a successful lawyer, civil rights advocate, and politician, was born in Richmond. He served as Virginia's lieutenant governor and, in 1990, became governor, the first African American elected to a governorship in U.S. history.

Colonial leaders established Middle Plantation in 1632 on a peninsula between the James and York Rivers. Settlers there escaped coastal mosquitoes, enjoyed richer soil for farming, and could better defend themselves from attack. In 1699, the House of Burgesses changed the name to WILLIAMSBURG to honor the king, William III, and made it the colony's capital. (Revolutionary leaders moved the capital to Richmond in 1780.) In 1926, concerned citizens launched a successful plan to preserve Williamsburg's historic buildings.

In 1693, King William III and his wife, Queen Mary II, granted a charter to establish THE COLLEGE OF WILLIAM & MARY. The school is the second oldest college in the United States, and it established the nation's first law school in 1779.

Town watchmen carried lanterns on their walks through Williamsburg every night. Each hour, their cry of "All's well!" assured citizens they were safe.

BOOKER T. WASHINGTON

(1856–1915) was born a slave on a tobacco farm near Roanoke. He was emancipated (freed) at age nine at the end of the Civil War. He studied to become a teacher, and in 1881 was named head of the Tuskegee Institute in Alabama. Washington worked throughout his life to create educational opportunities for African Americans.

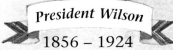

President Wilson
1856 – 1924

In order to save money on grass cutting during wartime, President Wilson let a flock of sheep graze on the White House lawn. Wilson sold their wool to raise money for the Red Cross.

THOMAS WOODROW WILSON

was born in Staunton in the Shenandoah Valley. He graduated from Princeton University and the University of Virginia School of Law, and received a doctorate in political science from Johns Hopkins University. Wilson became a professor and was appointed president of Princeton in 1902. He is interred in the National Cathedral, the only president laid to rest in the nation's capital.

28TH PRESIDENT (1913–1921)

★ Wilson was president during World War I.

★ A champion of world peace and democracy, he lead the effort to establish the League of Nations (a predecessor to the United Nations).

★ Wilson strongly supported the 19th amendment, which gave women the right to vote.

★ He suffered a stroke in 1919 and was an invalid for the rest of his presidential term.

★ He was awarded the Nobel Peace Prize in 1920.

X Y and Z

During Virginia's colonial period, **YORKTOWN** was a thriving port on the banks of the York River, just off the Chesapeake Bay. But Yorktown is best known for its role in the Revolutionary War.

In summer of 1781, after six long years of fighting, General George Washington was preparing for a battle in New York when he saw a chance to deliver a major blow to British forces. He learned that France was sending a large naval fleet to the Chesapeake Bay. France was Britain's enemy and, in 1778, had agreed to help America in its struggle for independence.

British General Lord Cornwallis and his troops were camped in Yorktown, to set up a navy base and await reinforcements. It took a month for Washington to march American and French soldiers from New York to Virginia. Meanwhile, when British ships arrived in September to help Cornwallis, the French fleet was there to meet them. In the Battle of the Virginia Capes (in the ocean off Cape Henry and Cape Charles) that followed, the French defeated the British. This secured the bay for the Americans, trapped Cornwallis, and assured he would not get reinforcements. Washington launched his attack early the next month. Cornwallis formally surrendered on October 19, 1781, effectively ending the war.

Yorktown never fully recovered from the battle. Today, it is part of the **COLONIAL TRIANGLE**, which includes Jamestown and Williamsburg.

Claiming to be sick, Cornwallis did not attend the surrender ceremony. His deputy brought Cornwallis's sword to give to Washington in a symbolic gesture of submission. Washington instructed one of his deputies to accept it.

In 1795, the United States approved a treaty with Great Britain that resolved many matters left over from the Revolutionary War. This angered France, who had been America's ally during the Revolution and who was then at war with Britain. The French began to capture U.S. ships carrying products for sale abroad, such as tobacco grown in Virginia.

President John Adams sent three diplomats, including Virginian John Marshall, to France to negotiate an end to the conflict. While there, three French agents approached them and demanded bribes and also loans to France in exchange for a settlement. The Americans said no, and when their reports were published in 1798, the French agents' names were kept secret—they were referred to only as "X, Y and Z."

The scandal became known as the **XYZ Affair** and brought the two countries to the verge of war. But Adams sent new diplomats to France and they eventually achieved a peaceful solution.

President Adams was so angry at the French he even asked George Washington to come out of retirement at Mount Vernon to command American forces.

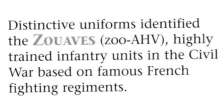

Distinctive uniforms identified the **Zouaves** (zoo-AHV), highly trained infantry units in the Civil War based on famous French fighting regiments.

The most famous Union Zouaves were the 11th New York Infantry Fire Zouaves, made up of New York City firefighters. They were organized in 1861 by the founder of the Zouave movement in the United States, Elmer E. Ellsworth.

At the onset of the war, Ellsworth transferred the New York Fire Zouaves to Washington to prepare to defend the capital. On May 24, 1861, the day after Virginia citizens voted to secede from the Union, Colonel Ellsworth led his unit into Alexandria. While on patrol, Ellsworth saw a Confederate flag waving from the top of an inn. He went up to the roof and cut it down. The angry innkeeper, a strong secessionist, shot and killed him. Ellsworth became the first Union officer to die in the Civil War.

Now that you have sampled Virginia's fascinating history, we hope you will want to learn more. We suggest below some sources that will help you begin. We also encourage you to travel throughout the Commonwealth, visiting the places where history was made and making new discoveries for yourself.

Here are some websites you will enjoy:

www.virginia.gov

www.virginia.org

www.eduplace.com/state/va/va_links

www.kidscommonwealth.virginia.gov/home

www.vahistorical.org/

Here are some books for reading and reference:

Bausum, Ann
Our Country's Presidents
National Geographic Society, 2001

Bobrick, Benson
Fight For Freedom: The American Revolutionary War
Atheneum Books, 2004

Bolotin, Norman
Civil War A to Z
Dutton, 2002

Bowman, John
The History of the American Presidency
World Publications Group, Inc., 2002

Coleman, Brooke
The Colony of Virginia
The Rosen Publishing Group, Inc., 2000

Edwards, Pamela Duncan
O is for Old Dominion: A Virginia Alphabet
Sleeping Bear Press, 2005

Harris, Bill
The First Ladies Fact Book
Black Dog & Leventhal Publishers, Inc., 2005

Kalman, Marsha E
Civil War A to Z
Random House, 2000

Katcher, Philip
Battle History of the Civil War, 1861–1865
Barnes & Noble, 2000

Pollack, Pamela
Virginia: The Old Dominion
World Almanac Library, 2002

Riehecky, Janet
The Settling of Jamestown
World Almanac Library, 2002

Rosen, Daniel
New Beginnings: Jamestown and the Virginia Colony, 1607–1699
National Geographic Society, *2005*

Smith, Karla
All Around Virginia: People of Virginia; Regions and Resources; Virginia History; Virginia Native Peoples; Virginia Plants and Animals; Uniquely Virginia
Heinemann, 2003